26.60

 P9-AQE-417

MARCO POLO

Please visit our web site at: www.worldalmanaclibrary.com
For a free color catalog describing World Almanac® Library's list of high-quality books
and multimedia programs, call 1-800-848-2928 (USA) or 1-800-387-3178 (Canada).
World Almanac® Library's fax: (414) 332-3567.

Library of Congress Cataloging-in-Publication Data

Gefen, Keren.
    Marco Polo / by Keren Gefen. — North American ed.
       p. cm. — (Great explorers)
    Includes bibliographical references and index.
    Summary: Discusses the life of the Venetian explorer and the book based on his
thirteenth-century travels along the Silk Road to the court of the Kublai Khan in China.
    ISBN 0-8368-5017-3 (lib. bdg.)
    ISBN 0-8368-5177-3 (softcover)
    1. Polo, Marco, 1254-1323?—Journeys—Juvenile literature. 2. Explorers—Italy—
Biography—Juvenile literature. 3. Voyages and travels—Juvenile literature. 4. Asia—
Description and travel—Juvenile literature. 5. Travel, Medieval—Juvenile literature.
[1. Polo, Marco, 1254-1323? 2. Explorers. 3. Voyages and travels. 4. Asia—
Description and travel.] I. Title. II. Great explorers (Milwaukee, Wis.)
G370.P9G44 2001
915.04'2—dc21
[B]   2001026813

This North American edition first published in 2002 by
World Almanac® Library
330 West Olive Street, Suite 100
Milwaukee, Wisconsin 53212 USA

This U.S. edition © 2002 by World Almanac® Library.
Created with original © 2001 by Quartz Editions,
112 Station Road, Edgware HA8 7AQ, U.K.
Additional end matter © 2002 by World Almanac® Library.

Series Editor: Tamara Green
World Almanac® Library editor and contributing writer: Gini Holland
World Almanac® Library project editor: Betsy Rasmussen
World Almanac® Library designer: Melissa Valuch

The creators and publishers of this volume wish to thank the following for their kind permission to feature
illustration material: Front cover: main image, Helen Jones/ other images: Bridgeman Art Archive, Bibliothèque
Nationale, Paris/ Bridgeman Art Library, Musée Guimet, Paris/ The Art Archive, Bibliothèque Nationale, Paris/
Mary Evans Picture Library/M. Louvet, Impact; Back cover: Bridgeman Art Library/ AKG, Musée Guimet, Paris/
AKG, Museo Civico Correr, Venice/ AKG, Bibliothèque Nationale, Paris/ Bodleian Library , Oxford/ Tony Stone
Images; 5 t Bridgeman Art Library, Bibliothèque Nationale, Paris/ c Bridgeman Art Library, Musée Guimet, Paris/
b Mary Evans Picture Library; 6 t The Art Archive/ c Bridgeman Art Library, Museo Correr, Venice/ b The Art
Library; 7 Helen Jones; 8 t Ancient Art & Architecture Collection/ b The Art Archive, Bibliothèque Nationale,
Paris/ 10 t Bridgeman Art Archive, Bibliothèque Nationale, Paris/ c Bodleian Library, Oxford/ b The Art Archive,
Bibliothèque Nationale, Paris; 11 t, c Tony Stone Images/ b Impact; 14 Tony Stone Images; 15 t, b AKG; 16 t
Bodleian Library, Oxford/ c, t Tony Stone Images/ c, b The Art Archive, Musée Condé, Chantilly/ b Bridgeman
Art Library, Bibliothèque Nationale, Paris; 17 t The Art Archive/ b Tony Stone Images; 18 t Bodleian Library,
Oxford/ b Bridgeman Art Library, Johannesburg Art Gallery; 19 t Bridgeman Art Library, British Library, London/
c, b Bodleian Library, Oxford; 20 Bridgeman Art Library; 21 Bodleian Library, Oxford; 22 t Werner Forman
Archive, Museo Correr, Venice/ b Bridgeman Art Library; 23 t Impact/ b The Art Library, Bibliothèque Nationale,
Paris; 24 t Bridgeman Art Library/ c Ancient Art & Architecture Collection/ b Bodleian Library; 25 Bridgeman
Art Library; 26 t Bridgeman Art Library, Bibliothèque Nationale, Paris/ b Mary Evans Picture Library; 27 t Robert
Harding Picture Library/ c Bodleian Library, Oxford/ b, Bridgeman Art Library; 28 t Bridgeman Art Library,
Makins Collection/ b Bridgeman Art Library; 30 t Bridgeman Art Library/ b The Art Archive, Bibliothèque
Nationale, Paris; 32, 33 t Bodleian Library, Oxford; 33 b, 34 t Mary Evans Picture Library/ b Bridgeman Art
Library, Topkapi Palace Museum, Istanbul; 35 t Bridgeman Art Library, Bibliothèque Nationale, Paris/ c
Bridgeman Art Library/ b AKG, Museo Correr, Venice; 36 t The Art Archive/ c Bridgeman Art Library, Museo
Correr, Venice/ b Bridgeman Art Library; 38 t Tony Stone Images/ b P. Patenall; 39 t Croatian Tourist Board/ b
The Art Archive, Golestan Palace, Teheran; 40 Tony Stone Images; 42 Bridgeman Art Library, Bibliothèque
Nationale, Paris; 43 Helen Jones

All rights reserved. No part of this book may be reproduced, stored in a retrieval system, or transmitted in any
form or by any means, electronic, mechanical, photocopying, recording, or otherwise, without the prior written
permission of the copyright holder.

Printed in the United States of America

1 2 3 4 5 6 7 8 9 06 05 04 03 02

MARCO
POLO

KEREN GEFEN

PROPERTY OF
INDIAN TRAILS
PUBLIC LIBRARY

WORLD ALMANAC® LIBRARY

CONTENTS

INTRODUCTION

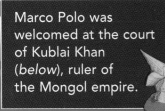

Marco Polo carried cargo by sea (*above*) and by camel to trade for other commodities.

Marco Polo met people of different religions, including those who worship Buddha (*right*).

Marco Polo was welcomed at the court of Kublai Khan (*below*), ruler of the Mongol empire.

MARCO POLO dared to explore Asian lands that held mystery to Europeans of the time. By doing so, he gave the world a book filled with vivid descriptions of the Asian places he visited and the Asian people he met.

MARCO POLO was born into a wealthy family of merchants in Venice, Italy. In 1269, he traveled with his father and uncle to meet Kublai Khan, the great Mongol Emperor. For the next 25 years, Polo completed many expeditions for Kublai Khan, collecting for him information and valuables from many regions of Asia, including China.

After Polo returned to Venice, his exploration experiences were published in a book that was widely read. People of his own time, however, did not believe all the accounts of his travels and questioned his integrity.

We now know that Polo did triumph as an explorer. He may well have been the first European to see some of Asia's most intriguing places. His close contact with various Asian people allowed him to learn about and appreciate cultures and traditions different from his own, and he then shared those experiences with other Europeans, giving the Western world its first glimpse of Eastern cultures.

Marco Polo (*above*) at age 12, from a copy of his book printed about 1500.

In his travels, Polo (*left*) met people from many different cultures, such as the Tatars, who lived in southern Russia.

MARCO POLO

MERCHANT AND TRAVELER

Remembered today for his journeys across Asia and his book describing them, Marco Polo claimed to have visited more places than anyone else before.

Marco Polo was born in the Italian city of Venice in 1254. His family were rich and successful merchants who were well respected in the community. They owned a fine house in Venice. They also owned shops and warehouses in the busy port of Korcula (now in Croatia) and in the international trading center at Sudak, on the northern shores of the Black Sea.

Like other Venetian merchants, men from the Polo family spent most of their time traveling. They journeyed east to meet traders from Arabia, Syria, Persia (now Iran), Iraq, and many Central Asian countries. These traders brought valuable goods, such as silks, jewels, and spices, from India and China to sell to Europeans.

In 1260, when Polo was six, his father Niccolò and his uncle Maffeo set off on one of their regular business trips — but disaster struck. They became trapped between enemy armies in a civil war. Meanwhile, back home in Venice, Polo's mother died. Polo's aunt cared for him and hired tutors to teach him. His father's servants helped him learn how to run the family

Venice, Italy (*right*), controlled shipping in the Mediterranean Sea during Polo's life. The citizens there grew rich by trading with Byzantium (now the city of Istanbul), Central Asia, and the Middle East.

> 66 *My book is dedicated to all people wishing to know the various races of men and peculiarities of various regions of the world.* 99

business. No one, however, could tell him when, or if, his father would return.

Polo heard nothing from his father or uncle for years. He was 15 years old when, amazingly, the two returned to Venice safe and well. They had an extraordinary story to tell. A Mongol nobleman had helped them escape from the civil war, and they had traveled with him to China to meet the Mongol emperor Kublai Khan, who was the most powerful ruler in the world. They planned to go back to China as soon as they could. Kublai Khan had asked them to bring some Christian preachers and some holy oil to his court. Most exciting of all was Polo's father's plan to take Polo with them.

By the time Polo (*right*) became an adult, he was well trained as a merchant. He could keep accounts, plan a journey, and read and write French and Italian.

The Polos' house in Venice, Italy (*right*), has survived for over 700 years. Like the homes of other merchants, it also served as a shop for selling valuable goods and as a warehouse for storing them.

This illustration (*below*) comes from one of Polo's earliest books and shows Marco Polo, his father, and his uncle saying goodbye as they set off on their journey to China in 1271.

GOING TO CHINA

It was three years before Niccolò, Maffeo, and Marco Polo were able to leave for China, but late in 1271, they set off. At the start of their journey, two Christian scholars traveled with them, but they turned back as soon as they came to a war zone.

To get to China, the Polos followed a network of rough pathways and camel tracks, known as the "Silk Road." The Silk Road had been used by merchants for over 1,000 years. It led them through Armenia, Georgia, Persia, and Afghanistan. It led them over the Pamir Mountains and across the Gobi and Taklamakan deserts. The three finally arrived at Kublai Khan's capital city of Shangdu. Their journey had taken three years.

Emperor Kublai Khan remembered Niccolò and Maffeo, and he welcomed them back to his court. He also greeted Marco warmly. Recognizing Marco Polo's intelligence, the khan offered

The Mongols were from Central Asia. During the 13th century, they conquered a vast empire, stretching from Hungary to Korea. In Kublai Khan's reign (1279–1294), the Mongols took control of China, which at that time had the most advanced civilization in the world.

> *If this young man lives, he will certainly become someone of great knowledge and worth.*
>
> KUBLAI KHAN

him a job. He already had many foreigners working for him in China. He trusted them to follow his orders more faithfully than the Chinese, whom he had conquered.

Marco spent the next 17 years working for Kublai Khan. He was sent on many fact-finding missions throughout China and the neighboring lands, and he served as a senior tax inspector. His father and uncle also worked for the Mongol empire, helping army engineers design war machines. The khan paid the Polos well for their services, and they became quite rich.

In 1290, the Polos started to think about returning to Europe. Kublai Khan was old and ill, and they feared that

the next Mongol ruler might not be so friendly. At first, the khan would not let them go, but he needed men he could trust to escort a Mongol princess to Persia. In 1292, the Polos left China forever.

RETURNING HOME

The journey back was terrible. They traveled by sea, because the Silk Road was blocked by wars. It took two years to reach Persia, sailing across the China Sea and Indian Ocean. They did not reach their own homes in Venice until 1295. Their family had given them up for dead long ago.

This was not the end of Polo's adventures, however. Three years later, fighting against Venice's rival city Genoa, he was captured and put in prison. There he met Rusticello, a well-known writer of romantic tales. Polo told Rusticello stories about his travels, and, after his release, Rusticello wrote these tales down in a book.

Polo was released from prison in 1299 and spent the rest of his life with his family. He married and had three daughters.

TIME LINE

1254
Marco Polo is born in Venice, Italy.

1260
Polo's father and uncle travel to the Black Sea and are trapped by a civil war. They head east to China.

1269
Polo's father and uncle return to Venice after meeting Mongol Emperor Kublai Khan.

1271
Polo leaves for China with his father and uncle.

1274 (or 1275)
The Polos reach Kublai Khan in China.

1275-1292
Polo is employed by the khan and travels in China.

1292
The Polos start their journey home and escort a princess to Persia.

1295
The Polos reach Venice.

1298
Polo is captured in war.

1298-1299
Polo meets writer Rusticello in prison, and together they plan a book describing Polo's travels.

1324
Polo dies at age 70.

THE SILK ROAD

The Silk Road linked Asia and Europe for over 1,000 years. It helped international trade to prosper and encouraged the spread of new ideas.

In Polo's time, travel by sea (*above*) was often easier than land travel, because there were no paved roads, few bridges or signs, and bandits along the way.

Where the Silk Road passed through deserts, travelers rode on camels, rather than horses or mules (*below*), because camels could survive in dry conditions.

From about 500 B.C., scholars, religious teachers, and government officials had walked, ridden animals, or traveled in carts along the network of tracks known as the Silk Road. Their mission was to trade goods and set up contacts between countries in Europe and Asia.

As far as we know, the earliest travelers along the Silk Road were Chinese, making the journey from east to west. From about A.D. 400, monks traveled from India along the Silk Road, bringing Buddhism to China. After the year 800, Muslims from the Middle East used the same route to introduce Islam to Central Asia. The first known European to travel the full length of the Silk Road was a Christian preacher named Giovanni de Piano Carpini. He journeyed from Italy to Mongolia in 1245, more than 25 years before Marco Polo.

In 1271, Marco Polo was still among the first Europeans to travel along the Silk Road,

heading east, from Europe to China. The long journey he made was unusual. Often, merchants only traveled short distances, from one big city to another. There they would meet buyers and sellers from several different lands.

SILK ROAD CITIES

By Marco Polo's time, many cities along the Silk Road had become busy international trading centers. Merchants built warehouses and showrooms in these cities, where they could display their goods in covered stalls.

In these cities, the merchants also bought foreign currency from money changers. They hired guides, interpreters, and armed escorts in preparation for the next stage of their journeys. They stocked up with essential supplies. They met to eat, drink, and arrange business deals at inns or rest houses called caravanserais.

Caravanserais provided merchants with a place to sleep and wash, as well as stabling for horses, camels, and mules. Caravanserais also provided secure storage for a merchant's goods.

MOUNTAIN HEIGHTS

To reach China, Polo had to travel over high mountain ranges, such as the Pamirs, in Afghanistan. He faced extreme cold, steep slopes, and a shortage of oxygen. Polo noticed the effects of this oxygen shortage, and he wrote that fires did not burn brightly and food did not cook well, but he did not understand the scientific reasons behind it.

WIDE OPEN SPACES

Much of northeast Asia is a vast, treeless, windswept plateau covered with rough prairie grass. The temperature there is often bitterly cold. In Marco Polo's time, it was home to the Mongol people. Like Mongols today (*below*), they were nomads, who lived in yurts — movable houses

ROUGH GOING

made from felt spread over a wooden frame. The Mongols were expert horse riders and fierce warriors. They survived by raising horses, sheep, and goats.

DREADFUL DESERTS

Polo's route east along the Silk Road passed through some of the most inhospitable country in the world, including the stony Taklamakan Desert. In the local language of Turki, Taklamakan means "go there and you won't come out again." Many travelers in the Taklamakan reported seeing mirages. These mirages tempted travelers to stray from their planned route and become hopelessly lost.

Polo reported that other deserts (*above*) were equally threatening. He said some were haunted by voices, which howled in the night. In others, sand shifted in constantly blowing winds, confusing and disorienting travelers by instantly covering their footprints.

DID YOU KNOW?

From its eastern end at Xian, China, to its western end on the coast of the Mediterranean Sea, the Silk Road measured more than 3,000 miles (4,800 kilometers) long. At many points along the way, it was joined by smaller paths leading to important trading cities.

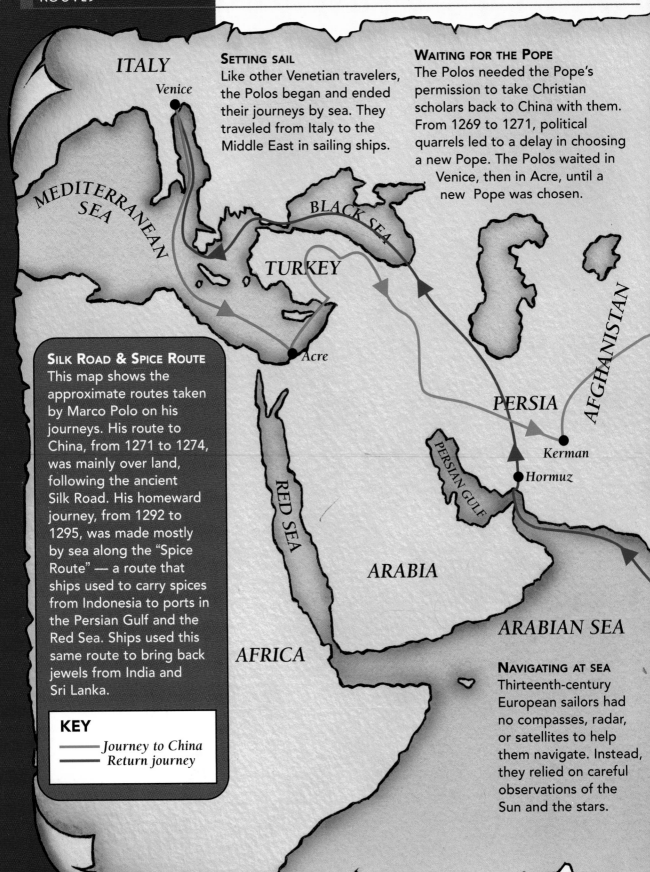

ITALY
Venice

SETTING SAIL
Like other Venetian travelers, the Polos began and ended their journeys by sea. They traveled from Italy to the Middle East in sailing ships.

WAITING FOR THE POPE
The Polos needed the Pope's permission to take Christian scholars back to China with them. From 1269 to 1271, political quarrels led to a delay in choosing a new Pope. The Polos waited in Venice, then in Acre, until a new Pope was chosen.

MEDITERRANEAN SEA

BLACK SEA

TURKEY

AFGHANISTAN

SILK ROAD & SPICE ROUTE
This map shows the approximate routes taken by Marco Polo on his journeys. His route to China, from 1271 to 1274, was mainly over land, following the ancient Silk Road. His homeward journey, from 1292 to 1295, was made mostly by sea along the "Spice Route" — a route that ships used to carry spices from Indonesia to ports in the Persian Gulf and the Red Sea. Ships used this same route to bring back jewels from India and Sri Lanka.

Acre

PERSIA

Kerman

PERSIAN GULF

Hormuz

RED SEA

ARABIA

ARABIAN SEA

AFRICA

KEY
— Journey to China
— Return journey

NAVIGATING AT SEA
Thirteenth-century European sailors had no compasses, radar, or satellites to help them navigate. Instead, they relied on careful observations of the Sun and the stars.

MARCO POLO'S TRAVELS

Karakorum

MONGOLIA

Shangdu

Dadu

GOBI DESERT

TAKLAMAKAN
DESERT

CHINA

TIBET

Chengdu

Hangzhou

MOUNTAINS, DESERTS, AND JUNGLES
Polo had to survive many harsh,
dangerous environments on his
travels — high mountains in Tibet,
deserts in East Asia, and jungles
in Burma and Vietnam.

Xiamen

BURMA

INDIA

BAY OF BENGAL

SOUTH CHINA SEA

VIETNAM

SRI LANKA

INDIAN OCEAN

SUMATRA

TRADE AND TREASURES

Asian spices (*below*), such as cloves, cinnamon, nutmeg, and ginger, were highly prized for flavoring foods and as medicines.

Silk-making was invented by the Chinese about 3000 B.C., but they kept the process a secret, encouraging foreigners to believe that silk grew on trees. Polo reported that silk thread (*below*) was really spun by silkworms.

International trade was a risky business, but merchants like Marco Polo ventured far and wide in the hope of making a fortune by bringing back treasures to sell.

Long journeys by land or sea were always hard and often dangerous. Travelers had to face bandits, pirates, slave-traders, and other dishonest people. They might meet tricksters trying to cheat them or fall victim to thieves, who raided the shops in towns.

Death was a real possibility. Marco Polo reported that many of his traveling companions were killed by Kurdish robbers in the north of Iraq. He included many warnings about "lawless men" in his book, so that future travelers could take care.

He also warned about health hazards. He noted, for example, that water from springs in the Persian desert was green and bitter. Just one small sip led to violent stomach upsets.

> *Wonderful rubies are to be found on this island [Sri Lanka] . . . there are also sapphires, topazes, amethysts, garnets and many other precious stones.*

Travelers might also catch diseases. Polo himself fell ill with malaria, which is caused by bites from mosquitoes carrying a parasite. He recovered after several months of rest in Afghanistan's cool mountain air.

RICH AND RARE

In spite of all these dangers, merchants still traveled the Silk Road, and they made expeditions away from its main route in order to explore the countries through which it passed. They were prepared to risk their lives in the hope of earning great wealth.

The goods European and Middle Eastern merchants traded for were rare and exotic, and therefore very valuable. Silk made in China was the best-known commodity, but European and Middle Eastern customers also demanded jewels, spices, medicines, pottery, and carpets. In return, European and Middle Eastern merchants exchanged wool cloth, dried fruits, Mediterranean coral, and glass.

COINS AND PAPER MONEY

Merchants usually paid for goods by bartering, but if they had nothing that they wanted to part with, they used silver and gold coins. Dinars, a type of money issued by powerful Muslim rulers in the Middle East, was a widely respected currency, but Polo usually used ducats, a gold and silver coinage minted in his home town of Venice.

When travelers reached the borders of Kublai Khan's empire, they were forced by Mongol government officials to change some of their coins into paper money. Paper money was a Mongol invention, and the khan wanted it used through-out his lands. In many ways, paper money was easier to use than gold or silver. It was much lighter to carry and did not jingle as travelers moved around. It was less durable, however, and not trusted or accepted every-where, even though harsh punishments were given by the khan to people who refused to use it.

FROM CHINA

While working for Kublai Khan, Marco Polo visited southeastern China, a region famous for its fine pottery. In his book, Polo admiringly described bright blue pots with a brilliant sheen. Chinese potters imported cobalt from the Middle East to make glazes for elegant vases and bowls. This vase (*right*) is decorated with a dragon, a traditional Chinese symbol of long life and royal power.

FROM INDIA

Marco Polo visited India twice and commented in his book on all the different spices grown there. Many of these spices were exported to China, where they were used locally or sold to traveling merchants (*below*). Polo reported that 43 cartloads of pepper grown in India were sold in the Chinese city of Hangzhou every day. Each cartload weighed 223 pounds (101 kilograms).

Polo explained how pearls were collected from oyster shells (*below*) along the east coast of India. Divers (*right*) held their breath as they swam down to the seabed to gather the oysters.

In Sumatra, Indonesia, Polo claimed to have seen a unicorn (*below*), but it was probably just a rhinoceros.

This picture (*right*) comes from a 15th-century copy of Polo's book. It shows a ship carrying an elephant and a camel. The artist has shown the animals to be almost as big as the ship.

TALES FROM TRAVELERS

It was natural for merchants to try to impress the people they met with tales of strange sights, marvels, and mysteries that they had seen on their journeys. Some of these tales were accurate, but others were false and invented only to deceive or entertain. Merchants had to be shrewd to judge whether or not a story was true. They did not want to waste time searching for imaginary countries or treasures. It was not always easy to see the truth, though. Even Marco Polo had been tricked into believing some fantastic stories.

MEN OR MONSTERS?

Polo's book assures readers that he had heard true reports of men with faces like dogs who lived on the Andaman Islands in the Indian Ocean, and other reports of men with tails, from Sumatra, Indonesia. Polo also repeated certain tales about huge stones that moved by themselves in Central Asia, chickens with fur instead of feathers in China, and magicians with the power to stop sharks from biting in India. Polo also described such things as bamboo, coconuts, oil wells, kites, and elephants, all things that most Europeans had never seen.

Once merchants returned to Europe, these exciting tales helped sell the items they brought back. Eager customers did not really care whether or not the stories were true.

FIT FOR A KING

Precious stones from China, India, and nearby lands were the most

valuable items brought to Europe by merchants. Diamonds, rubies, sapphires, and topazes were used to create beautiful jewelry, robes, and crowns. Most important of all, precious stones were used to decorate the covers of holy books and crosses displayed in churches.

Monarchs, the nobility, and church leaders were also the chief consumers of silks, spices, and other luxury goods carried to Europe along the Silk Road. These were the only people rich enough to afford them.

COLLECTING DIAMONDS

Marco Polo's book contains several accounts of the different ways gold and precious stones were collected by local people for selling to traveling merchants. One of the most extraordinary tales is about diamond collecting in southern India. Polo claimed that people from India used eagles to help them collect diamonds from a steep valley that was infested by

Polo wrote about a ruby belonging to the King of Sri Lanka. Polo believed the ruby to be the greatest in the world. It was as big as a man's hand and as thick as a man's arm, and "glowing red like fire." He offered to buy it but was refused.

poisonous snakes. The Indian people threw raw meat into the valley, and diamonds stuck to the meat. Eagles flew down, snatched up the meat, and then flew up out of the valley. The Indian people chased the eagles and took the diamond-covered meat from them.

DEADLY PERFUME

Polo also described how other valuable goods were obtained. On his visit to Tibet, for example, Polo saw musk deer. Musk, a heavy scent produced as a sticky liquid by a gland in the musk deer's abdomen, was a favorite ingredient in perfumes.

The Tibetans trained dogs to hunt and catch the deer. The hunters then killed the deer and collected the musk-producing glands.

Polo claimed he heard stories about people from India who used eagles (*above*) to help them collect diamonds.

Tales were told about the different ways people collected diamonds (*below*) for trade. Polo passed along some of these tales in his book.

 In a certain city, all the men had an entire set of capped, gold teeth, but the women's teeth were natural.

From Muslim storytellers in Central Asia and the Middle East, Polo heard tales of a Paradise Garden here on Earth (*above*), instead of in heaven.

PEOPLE, PLACES, AND IDEAS

As Marco Polo traveled, he encountered many civilizations, customs, and religions that were unfamiliar to him. He found them intriguing and amazing.

When Marco Polo left Venice, he was not completely ignorant of other lands. As they traveled to meet Kublai Khan, his father and uncle taught him about their earlier adventures. No tales, however, could substitute for his firsthand experiences. Polo's book makes it clear that he was astonished and excited by all the different things he saw when he began his journey.

Like other Europeans, he had little idea about the many different people and the many different lifestyles there were in the world. Describing the far south of India, for example, he wrote that "everything there is different from ours, and is bigger and more beautiful."

THE PEOPLE

Polo was curious about the appearances of people, and he described their clothing, hair, facial features, and physiques in detail. He recorded the Mongol custom of wearing two robes in winter — one with

To his surprise, Polo found communities of Christian men and women living on the west coast of India. Local traditions told how the Christian faith had been brought there by St. Thomas (*left*).

> **In Alaodin's Paradise, every kind of fruit grew in the gardens, while fresh water, milk, wine and honey flowed in the streams.**

Polo did not think it wise to believe reports from Madagascar about a monstrous rukh bird (*left*). It was said to be strong enough to carry an elephant.

the fur turned in and one with the fur turned out — as protection against the bitter cold. He also noticed the loincloths worn by people living in hot countries, such as India, commenting that they had no need for clothing in the heat.

In Yunnan, China, Polo observed people with gold-capped teeth and tattooed skin. In Ethiopia, he met Africans with faces decorated by patterns of scars, and he reported that this was considered "a badge of dignity."

He admired women he saw in southern China and Kashmir, commenting that the Kashmiri women were very beautiful. In Afghanistan, he was surprised to see women wearing trousers — this was unheard of in Europe during this time. He said the trousers were very full and pleated to give the impression of wide hips, because plumpness was fashionable and admired by Afghan husbands.

In men, Polo admired strength, bravery, and skill. He praised Mongol men as "tough fighters, excelling in bravery and courage." He said Mongol men were "the best in the world at making strenuous efforts and enduring hardship."

The European artist who drew this illustration (*above*) had no idea what non-European people looked like.

In this picture (*right*), a 15th-century European artist incorrectly showed people from Asia wearing European-style robes, instead of their own clothing styles.

NEW BELIEFS, NEW IDEAS

On his travels, Marco Polo came into contact with many religious ideas that were unfamiliar to him. Some were ancient, such as Zoroastrianism, founded in Persia around 1000 B.C., and Hinduism, which originated in India about 2000 B.C. Zoroastrians worshiped *Ahura Mazda*, meaning "Wise Lord." Hindus honored *Brahman*, meaning "Spirit." The traditional faith of the Mongol people was also ancient. The Mongol people prayed to *Tengri*, or "God of

heaven," and *Itugan*, or "Goddess of growing things." In India and Sri Lanka, Marco Polo met disciples of Buddha, the "Enlightened One," who was a religious leader who lived around 500 B.C.

In China, Polo met followers of two wise teachers, Kongfuzi (also called Confucius) and Laozi (also called Lao-tzu). Kongfuzi and Laozi had lived in the 6th century B.C. Buddhists, Confucians, and followers of Laozi did not worship any god, but instead followed the

good example set by their leaders.

Only one faith, Islam, was fairly new at the time. Islam was first preached by the Prophet Muhammad around A.D. 600. By Polo's time, it had spread from Arabia through Asia, North Africa, and the Middle East. Muslims prayed to *Allah*, meaning "God," and claimed kinship in religion with Jews and Christians, honoring Abraham, Moses, and Jesus.

In Marco Polo's time, Christian leaders in Europe were mostly intolerant of other faiths. Polo, however, remained open-minded and did not criticize or condemn. Instead, he was always curious and interested in learning more.

In Persia, Marco Polo saw temples and altars (*below*) where followers of the ancient Zoroastrian religion met to pray and meditate in front of holy fires. The fires were the symbol of their faith.

In some societies that Polo visited, there were no doctors. Instead, magicians would try to heal the sick by dancing, in order to try to remove evil spirits from a patient's body. Rams were also sometimes sacrificed to help with removing evil from ill patients.

In Sumatra, Polo claimed to have discovered a secret about how "monsters" were made (*below*). The locals dried a dead monkey and trimmed its fur so that it looked almost human.

Polo was impressed by the citizens of Hangzhou, China. He wrote that they were peace-loving, hard-working, honest, hospitable people, devoted to their families and always ready to welcome foreigners with kind advice.

Polo did not like all the people he met, however. He described the people of Tajikistan, for example, as "out and out bad." Although he criticized behavior when it shocked or annoyed him, he did not seem to be prejudiced against any ethnic, religious, or cultural group.

DIFFERENT LIFESTYLES

Polo also described the various lifestyles of people he met on his travels. In the Middle East, for example, where few plants grow in the hot, dusty deserts, farmers cultivated dates, cotton, sugar-cane, oranges, and apricots in oases. In India, he wrote that he passed through villages where people grew rice and wove some of "the finest cloth in the world."

After Polo went to Central Asia, he remarked that the women did all the hard work,

leaving the men free to spend their time hunting or fighting. Polo also noted that each Mongol man could have many wives and that they all lived together in "harmony and unity beyond praise."

In China, Polo was amazed at the size, richness, and sophistication of the cities, with their stone walls, paved streets, wide bridges, and beautiful parks and lakes. He admired the orderly way in which these cities were run, with fresh water supplies, well-stocked markets, night-watchmen, and fire brigades.

Polo admired Buddhist teachings and the Buddha's own holy life. He suggested that if Buddha had been a Christian, he would have been a saint.

Polo described a famous tomb for a king of Burma and said it was built "as a sign of his greatness and for the good of his soul." Polo's description inspired a 15th-century European artist to paint this picture (*right*).

Over the centuries, Marco Polo has become a symbol linking civilizations in Europe and Asia. This statue of him (*left*) was crafted by an Asian artist.

INTERNATIONAL AMBASSADORS

After he arrived at Kublai Khan's court, Marco Polo was trusted with diplomatic and fact-finding missions intended to help protect and expand the Mongol Empire.

During wars between Christians and Muslims in the Middle East, peaceful merchant ships, like this one (*below*), were attacked in the Mediterranean Sea.

Polo's father and uncle first met Kublai Khan around 1265 when they traveled east with a Mongol nobleman to escape wars in Central Asia. They were pleased and rather surprised when Kublai Khan welcomed them to his court. The Polos had expected to be given food and shelter, because hospitality to travelers was an honored tradition in most parts of the world. They also expected curiosity, suspicion, and maybe even hostility from the khan and his people because of their unfamiliar looks and speech. The Polos claimed that they were the first western Europeans the khan had ever seen. This may not be true, but Kublai Khan certainly did not know much about civilizations west of the Black Sea.

The Church of the Holy Sepulcher at Jerusalem (*left*). Christians believe Jesus was buried on this site where the church now stands. The khan asked for oil from lamps kept burning there.

INTERESTED IN LEARNING

Kublai Khan was an intelligent man with interests in many things. Unlike early Mongol conquerors, he had taken the trouble to learn about the cultures, beliefs, and traditions of the different people living in the lands he ruled, especially the ancient Chinese civilization.

The khan invited thinkers, scholars, artists, and religious leaders from all parts of his empire to visit him at his court. He questioned them about their ideas, and he admired their achievements. When Marco Polo's father and uncle arrived unexpectedly at Kublai Khan's court, he realized that this was his chance to learn about European lands and the Christian faith.

The khan's mother had belonged to a small and little-known branch of the Christian Church in East Asia. Over the centuries it had lost touch with the rest of the Christian world. So the khan asked the Polos to go back to Europe and take friendly greetings to the Pope. He hoped the Pope would send him 100 Christian scholars and preachers, so that he and the other religious men already staying at his court could find out more about Christianity. As a great collector of treasures of all kinds, the khan also asked the Polos to bring him a special, holy gift — some oil from the lamps burning in the church built on the site where Jesus was buried, near Jerusalem.

A POLITICAL PURPOSE

Kublai Khan had another reason for welcoming the Polos. He wanted to make an alliance with European leaders against Muslim rulers in the Middle East. For over 200 years, there had been wars, known to Christians as the Crusades, in Middle Eastern lands. They were fought between Muslims and Christians for the territory around the city of Jerusalem. As is the case today, Jerusalem was a holy city to Muslims,

CHRISTIAN LEADER

- The **Pope** (*below, seated*) was the leader of Christians in western Europe and the head of the Roman Catholic Church. In Marco Polo's time, all European Christians were Roman Catholics — Protestant churches had not yet developed.

- In Marco Polo's time, popes were powerful political figures, as well as spiritual leaders. They ruled a large part of Italy and acted as advisors to European kings and princes. Between 1096 and 1291, the Popes urged Christian people to fight against Muslims for control of the "Holy Land" (a territory in the Middle East, near Jerusalem) in a series of wars called the Crusades.

- Pope Gregory X reigned from 1271 to 1276 and supported Polo's expedition east to meet Kublai Khan. The Pope wanted to make an alliance with the Mongols to help fight against Muslim armies in the Middle East.

One of Polo's crew members helps him load his ship in the lower part of this stained glass window (*below*).

Mongol soldiers (*above*) conquered a vast empire between A.D. 1200 and 1300. Armies loyal to rival Mongol leaders also fought each other.

A 15th-century European artist's view of Kublai Khan (*below right*) giving gold passports to Polo's father and uncle on their first visit to his court.

Jews, and Christians, and each mistrusted the religious beliefs of the others.

Religious differences, however, masked a deeper rivalry between powerful rulers in Europe and the Middle East. The Byzantines, who were Christians, ruled Greece, Turkey, Bulgaria, and islands in the Mediterranean Sea. The sultans, who were Muslims, ruled North Africa, Arabia, and many states in the Middle East. Both sides hoped to expand their empires and would fight if necessary.

THE CRUSADES

The Crusades began in 1096, when Christians invaded the Holy Land, which was ruled by Muslims. At first, Christian armies were successful, driving out Muslim sultans and setting up Christian kingdoms. Then the Muslims fought back.

By the 1260s, when the Polos first met Kublai Khan, the Christians were facing defeat.

Some Christian leaders hoped that the Mongols might help them fight against the Muslims. Other Christians, who feared the Mongol armies, thought the Mongol armies might try to invade Europe, as they had in the Middle East.

DANGEROUS ENEMIES

Far away in China, Kublai Khan felt the impact of these wars. Already, as the Mongol empire expanded westward across Asia, Mongol soldiers had clashed with Muslim troops as the Mongol army conquered many Muslim lands. Muslim rulers were fighting to win these lands back. The Muslims were also planning to attack eastern Europe, which the Mongols wanted for themselves. Kublai Khan hoped that the Pope and Christian rulers in Europe would join him to fight growing Muslim power.

Kublai Khan also wanted to monitor events in parts of the Mongol empire, such as southern Russia and Iraq, that were far away from his capital in Eastern Asia. The Mongol governors who ruled there were greedy for power and often fought among themselves. The khan thought that traveling merchants like the Polos could usefully serve as spies. He hoped they might also encourage the Pope and other European leaders to help the khan keep control of his empire if need be. The Polos had already learned that wars could seriously disrupt journeys and hinder trade.

Although Kublai Khan did not intend it, his friendship toward the Polos had another, equally important effect. In a small way, it helped increase knowledge and improve understanding between civilizations in eastern Asia and western Europe. The stories Polo told about his travels inspired wonder and curiosity among geographers and mapmakers for hundreds of years.

DID YOU KNOW?

Kublai Khan gave Polo's father and uncle a gold passport so that the officials could prove who they were and demand obedience. The passports were decorated with pictures. Many people of that time could not read, but they recognized the gold cards and could understand the pictures.

This French map of Asia (*below*) was made many years after Polo traveled. It shows Kublai Khan in his tent with the Polos to the right. Accurate maps and charts of land and sea had not been made in Marco Polo's time. The story of his travels from west to east was used to decorate many later maps.

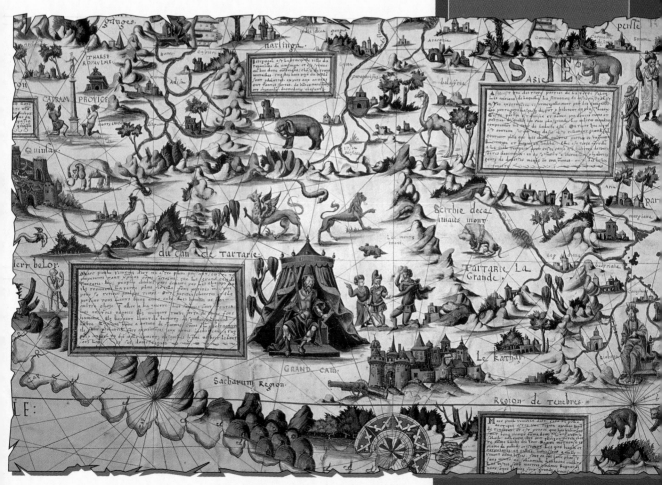

DANGEROUS JOURNEY

It took Marco Polo over three years to travel from Europe to China to meet Kublai Khan. He encountered delays and dangers along the way.

Mongol soldiers attacking a walled city (*above*). Armed guards, gathered on top of the walls, shoot arrows and hurl javelins at the Mongols, hoping to drive them away.

A 13th-century manuscript from Persia shows this group (*right*) traveling safely through Mongol lands to the holy city of Mecca, Arabia.

In 1271, Polo, his father, and his uncle collected holy oil from Jerusalem and set out for Kublai Khan's court. Two Christian preachers traveled with them. This was far fewer than the 100 religious scholars the khan had asked for, but not many priests were willing to volunteer for such a risky journey. The Polos also carried gifts of gold and crystal from the Pope, as tokens of friendship toward the khan.

Their journey began well, but within weeks, the Polos had run into danger. When they reached southern Turkey, they found that the Muslim ruler of Egypt was attacking there. Polo described how he feared for his life and how the two Christian preachers decided to travel no further and returned home. The three Polo men decided to go on.

"THE MONGOL PEACE"

Battles, sieges, invading armies, rampaging soldiers, and other chaos of war were some of the greatest dangers faced by travelers in Asia and the Middle East.

In some ways, Marco Polo was fortunate to travel when he did. The years from 1200 to 1300 are sometimes called "the Mongol Peace." By the 1270s, when Polo made his long journey east to China, Mongol armies had conquered so much territory in Central Asia that China and neighboring lands were safer than ever before. Mongol governors enforced harsh laws, and Mongol soldiers were stationed close to large cities and towns, ready to put down any lawlessness or rebellion.

SCORCHED EARTH

Although it was safer, it was often not very pleasant traveling through conquered lands. It was policy for the Mongols to destroy as much as possible when they took control of a kingdom. City walls were pulled down, houses and markets were smashed, stores were looted, crops were trampled in the fields, and sometimes whole towns were set on fire.

When Polo reached the once-rich city of Balkh, Afghanistan,

which had been recently attacked by the Mongols, he reported that many of its houses were "shattered now, and in ruins."

Mongol armies deliberately terrorized conquered people so that they would not rebel against Mongol control. Mongol soldiers were ruthless toward their enemies. Anyone who fought against Mongol attack and was captured would be executed. Their heads were cut off and used to build a grisly monument, known as a tower of skulls. People who did not resist Mongol invaders and surrendered peacefully were allowed to live under strict Mongol rule.

The Mongols attacked enemy cities with fearsome war-machines, such as this massive catapult (*below*).

This 13th-century Chinese painting (*right*) shows Mongol troops galloping across a bleak landscape after conquering the kingdom of Tibet. Marco Polo commented that Mongol invaders left many Tibetan towns and villages "ruined and desolate."

Marco Polo would have found an early Asian boat like this one (*above*) very unstable. He was fortunate not to have had to engage in a sea battle while in the service of Kublai Khan.

Kublai Khan (*left*) ruled from 1260 to 1294. Polo described him as of moderate height, with well-fleshed limbs, a ruddy complexion, black eyes, and a handsome nose.

The winds there blew across the desert sand, becoming so hot and dry that travelers jumped into any water they could find to avoid getting burned. Polo also told how an entire army that camped in the desert was killed by the dry, suffocating heat. Gruesomely, he added that the soldiers' bodies were so shriveled that they fell to pieces when people tried to bury them.

SNOW, RAIN, FLOODS

Bad weather was another travel hazard. In his book, Polo explained that his journey to meet Kublai Khan took so long because "snow, rain, and flooded rivers" made it impossible to travel in wintertime. Howling winds made it difficult to travel and to survive in camp.

KILLER HEAT

Summers could also be dangerous for travel. Polo described conditions on the shores of the Persian Gulf.

NO FOOD OR SHELTER

During the time Polo traveled, there were few settlements where travelers could find shelter. In uninhabited countryside, they had to camp in makeshift tents of canvas cloth or huddle under rocks or in caves. They had to take food and water with them, since often there was nothing to eat or drink along the way. Polo warned travelers entering the Gobi Desert that they needed enough supplies to last for a whole month.

Overnight stops to rest and feed animals could also be dangerous. Unless travelers kept a careful lookout, their camp might be attacked by wolves or lions while they slept.

Packhorses could die from eating poisonous herbs (many grew in northwest China) or drinking salty water. The loss of horses left travelers

DID YOU KNOW?

On the island of Andaman, Marco Polo found a group of people who were known to eat human flesh whenever they caught a foreigner. Polo felt lucky to escape from these cannibals with his life.

> **In Fu-chau, the citizens slay as many enemies as possible in battle, drink their blood, and then eat their flesh.**

stranded, with little chance of being rescued before collapsing from hunger or thirst.

ILL-EQUIPPED

Marco Polo had little equipment to help him survive. He and his companions had no truly waterproof clothes or boots and no warm sleeping bags. Instead, Polo, his father, and his uncle wrapped themselves in heavy robes of smelly leather, oiled cloth, and thick, bulky sheepskin or fur. Polo commented that people they met wearing similar clothes looked like beasts. Sometimes, nothing seemed warm enough. Polo claimed that cold weather in the high plateau land around Kerman,

Persia, was so intense that it could "scarcely be kept out by any number of furs."

Even lighting fires to keep warm might not be a simple task. There were no matches or portable stoves. Travelers struck a flint against steel to produce a spark, and they gathered wood for fuel when they could find it. In wet, cold weather, fires might not light at all.

SAFER BY SEA?

Transportation was not always safe, either. Ships, carts, camels, horses, and mules could all be unpredictable and unreliable. Polo told how he planned to travel by sea to India from the port of Ormuz in southern Persia and then on to China, but he did not trust the local ships after learning that their wooden hulls were sewn together with rope made of coconut fiber, instead of being securely fastened by iron nails. He also learned that travel by sea to China could be very risky. Ships often sank in Indian Ocean storms. Fearfully, the Polos headed back inland toward Pakistan and the Chinese frontier.

A CRUEL CUSTOM

Even if the weather was mild, the terrain easy-going, and the wildlife friendly, local traditions might present unexpected dangers to travelers. It was the custom for all powerful noblemen descended from Mongol Emperor Genghis Khan to be buried at Karakorum in Central Mongolia. This meant carrying their dead bodies for thousands of miles. All living creatures that met a nobleman's body on its final journey were killed, in order to serve its spirit in the world of the dead.

The Polos were lucky. They narrowly missed meeting the funeral procession of Barak, Mongol lord of Turkestan in western China. He died shortly before they traveled in 1270.

KUBLAI KHAN'S COURT

Genghis Khan (*above*), founder of the Mongol empire, ruled from 1206 to 1227 and was the grandfather of Kublai Khan.

This 15th-century European manuscript shows Marco Polo (*below, second from right*) kneeling respectfully as he greets Kublai Khan. His uncle kneels beside him while his father stands behind, introducing him to the khan.

Kublai Khan intended to make sure the Mongol empire was well run. With Marco Polo's help, the khan learned many new things about his empire.

Foreigners could not enter China without being observed, and Polo reported that Kublai Khan sent royal officials to meet the three Polo men while they were still 40 days traveling distance away from his court. The royal officials escorted the Polos as honored guests for the final stage of their long journey.

At last the Polos reached

> " *He has every right to be called the Great Khan as no man since Adam has ever ruled over so many subjects or over such a vast territory, nor has any ruler ever been possessed of such treasure or of such power.* "

Kublai Khan's palace at Shangdu, China. They were welcomed "with good cheer . . . mirth . . . and merry-making." The khan called them to meet him and asked many questions about their journey. They presented him with the gifts they had brought from the Pope and handed over the holy oil from Jerusalem. Kublai Khan was delighted and invited them all to stay at his court.

LORD OF LORDS

In his book, Polo explained that the title *khan* means "Great Lord of Lords." Born in 1215, Kublai Khan was about 60 years old and at the height of his power when Marco Polo first met him in 1275. He had proved himself as a soldier and was close to winning a long war to take control of Chinese lands.

A RICH INHERITANCE

Kublai Khan's grandfather, Genghis Khan, had founded the Mongol empire and conquered a vast territory, reaching from Mongolia to the Black Sea.

When Genghis Kahn died, his empire was divided among his four sons. The eastern part, which Kublai Khan ruled, was the largest and most powerful. Kublai Khan also oversaw the three smaller divisions of the empire — Central Asia, South Russia, and the Middle East.

BORN TO RULE

Kublai Khan was more than just a warrior, however. He was interested in a wide range of subjects, from philosophy to big-game hunting. His mother, a remarkable woman named Sorghagtani Beki, made sure he learned to read and write, unlike his Mongol ancestors. He was also a skilled administrator, keeping firm control of his empire and all its different traditions. To help, the khan recruited foreign advisors, like the Polos, so that his empire would benefit from their expertise. He also employed magicians and

KUBLAI KHAN'S LIFE

1215
Kublai Khan is born.

1253
Kublai Khan leads Mongol armies to capture Yunnan, in southeast China.

1259
Kublai Khan fights his brother for the right to be the next Mongol emperor. He wins and declares himself "Great Khan."

1271
Kublai Khan moves the capital of the Mongol empire from Karakorum, Mongolia, to Dadu. He takes the extra title of "Emperor of China."

1279
Kublai Khan's army completes a conquest of China. Mongol Yuan dynasty, founded by Kublai Khan, replaces Chinese Sung dynasty as rulers of all of China.

1277-1287
Kublai Khan's army conquers Vietnam and Burma.

1294
Kublai Khan dies.

Every year, Kublai Khan celebrated his birthday (September 28) with a lavish feast in his palace. A 15th-century European artist shows the khan (*left*) drinking from a gold cup and wearing a crown.

Polo reported that Kublai Khan was served by 12,000 members of a group of nobility called "keshikten." Each nobleman received gold belts and fine robes (*above*) as a sign of rank.

Kublai Khan's officials collected one-tenth of all cloth made in his empire, and it was used to provide clothes for poor families. They built up large stocks of grain and handed out free food to poor people (*right*) living in his capital — up to 30,000 bowls of rice or millet every day.

astronomers from India and Tibet. They claimed they could change the weather and foretell future events.

TRADITIONS

The Mongol people did not share the same traditions as the people they conquered. Mongol people lived nomad lifestyles, based on hunting, rearing animals, and warrior raids. The Chinese were very different. Their ancient and advanced civilization was based in cities and farms. They respected scholarship and the written word. Mongol arts and entertainments were rough and exuberant. The Chinese arts were delicate and refined. Chinese society was strictly organized, respecting ancestors

and men. Mongolian families were relaxed, and women had considerable power.

Helped by his mother, Kublai Khan learned how to manage Chinese people without provoking rebellion. He allowed the Chinese to continue their traditional culture and way of life so long as they obeyed the Mongol officials who controlled them.

GRAND PALACES

As a guest at the royal palace, Marco Polo was astounded by the magnificent style in which Kublai Khan lived. The khan had two main palaces, at Dadu (present-day Beijing) in winter and Shangdu (northern China) in summer. Both were large and sumptuous. The winter palace stood high on a hill and was surrounded by two sets of walls, for privacy and security, and beautiful parkland with tall trees and a lake. Inside, it was decorated with gold and silver. Outside, it was decorated with carvings and paintings in brilliant reds, yellows, and blues. Polo described the number of rooms in the palace as bewildering, and he claimed that the main hall was large enough to seat at least 6,000 guests. The khan's summer palace was equally impressive. Its design was based on a traditional Mongol tent but made of the costliest materials.

Kublai Khan had four official wives and many minor wives. We do not know how many children he fathered, but Polo suggested he had about 50 sons. The khan's favorite wife, Chabi, acted as an advisor. Sadly, Kublai Khan's favorite son, Zhen Jin, died while still very young.

Its walls were made of gilded and lacquered bamboo held in place by silken cords.

Inside each palace, Kublai Khan walked on priceless carpets and sat on thrones cushioned in silk. His private chambers were lined with soft silky fur and draped with tiger skins. He wore splendid robes of gold cloth, embroidered with silk and studded with jewels. His wives, courtiers, and servants were also richly dressed. Musicians, story-tellers, magicians, foreign visitors, and a full-grown pet lion entertained him.

CENTERS OF GOVERNMENT

Kublai Khan's palaces were more than splendid homes. They were also centers of government, where the khan met with army leaders and top officials to plan new campaigns. He kept a close watch on how the empire was run, receiving reports from police chiefs, watchmen, couriers, mail runners, tax collectors, market supervisors, and officials in charge of currency, weights, and measures. He also monitored the progress of his favorite building projects, such as the great canal, which linked Dadu with the rich farmlands of southern China.

Kublai Khan employed hunters, trackers, falconers, and grooms (*above*). With them, he went on expeditions to northern China, killing thousands of animals.

Polo reported that Kublai Khan liked to hunt. He sometimes used tame cheetahs, which rode behind him on horseback (*below*), to chase and catch different kinds of deer in the parkland surrounding his summer palace at Shangdu.

> ❝ *The Khan owes his throne to his spirit, his bravery, and superior intelligence.* ❞

EXPLORING THE EMPIRE

Marco Polo spent 17 years working for Kublai Khan. He visited many parts of the Mongol empire, making detailed reports of the things he saw.

In western China and Tibet, Marco Polo met skillful magicians, like this woman (*above*). They claimed to control the weather, creating rainstorms and thunder whenever they wished. In Yunnan, southern China, Polo met shamans who used magic to try to cure people who were ill.

Kublai Khan wanted to learn all he could about his empire, so he employed foreigners, such as Marco Polo, to carry out empire business and report on all the empire lands. He trusted foreigners more than people he had conquered to tell him the truth.

Polo noticed that the khan was angry when officials he had sent to distant parts of the Mongol empire could not provide a detailed account of the people and places they had seen. So, when Kublai Khan asked Polo to go on a business trip for him, Polo made sure that he observed and remembered all the interesting sights along the way.

CURIOSITIES

Kublai Khan was very pleased with Polo's report. From then on, Polo boasted that he "never ceased to travel on special missions and to bring back news of novelties and curiosities." These "curiosities" included everything from man-eating snakes (which may have been crocodiles) in southern China, to acrobatic temple-dancers in India.

Looking back over his long career serving Kublai Khan, Polo wrote that his journeys had lasted months, or even

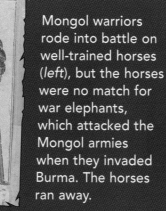

Mongol warriors rode into battle on well-trained horses (*left*), but the horses were no match for war elephants, which attacked the Mongol armies when they invaded Burma. The horses ran away.

years, and that he went to Tibet, southern China, Laos, Burma, Vietnam, Bengal (present-day Bangladesh and nearby lands), and the east coast of India.

HUMAN INTEREST

Everywhere Polo went, he took notice of the local governments, religions, homes, and foods.

In Hangzhou, the chief trading center of southern China and the largest city in the world at that time, Polo saw huge pears, weighing 10 pounds (4.5 kilograms)

each, that were "white as dough inside, and very fragrant." He also saw yellow and white peaches.

TECHNOLOGY AND TRADE

Polo described the different ways people made their livings, as well as the technology they acquired and the currency they used. He also took note of the kinds of rare and valuable goods they had to sell. He often commented on their appearances and any customs that were unfamiliar to him.

In southern China, he was shocked at meeting people who ate human flesh and "all sorts of brute beasts."

Kublai Khan gave orders for mulberry trees to be planted beside main roads across his empire. They guided travelers, and their leaves fed silkworms. Their bark (in bags, below) was used for paper.

Paper money (below) was accepted in most parts of the khan's empire, but Polo reported that Tibetans preferred to use salt as currency. In southern parts of the empire, valuable cowrie shells from the seas around Vietnam were used as currency.

Polo reported that many European merchants (left) came to Kublai Khan's empire to trade. In Dadu, there were separate hostels for the French, Germans, and Italians.

In southern China, Polo would have seen farmers pumping up water from ditches to their rice fields using an endless chain machine (*right*) — a Chinese invention first built around A.D. 100. Powered by two men stepping on pedals, wooden blades fixed to the endless chain constantly pushed a stream of water uphill.

Polo had seen tattooing in Europe (*below*), but he was amazed by the whole-body tattoos he saw in Laos. Every inch of the skin was covered.

EVERYDAY LIVES

Wherever possible, Polo reported on the ordinary lives of people. He watched everyone — from farmers and crafts people to priests, judges, and kings. In India, he met yogis who followed a pure, simple lifestyle. They claimed to live for over 150 years.

Polo also observed rank and status. He noted, for example, that men and women in Laos were tattooed — their skin covered with pictures of lions, dragons, and birds. Polo explained that this was a sign of nobility and beauty. The tattoo process was amazingly painful, and people often died from loss of blood.

UNFAMILIAR BELIEFS

Polo also reported on beliefs and customs that were unfamiliar to him. In India, for example, he was told that a sneeze was a bad omen for travelers and that certain hours of the day were unlucky. He said that in some Indian districts, wives and servants were expected to kill themselves when their husbands or masters died. In China, he was astonished to see paper models of houses, horses, and other valuable items burned at funerals,

Chinese farmers used oxen or water buffalo to pull heavy plows through the soil (*left*) and muscle power to thresh grains of wheat or millet from their stalks. Women worked alongside men in the fields.

Kublai Khan employed thousands of couriers to keep in touch with distant parts of his empire. They carried urgent messages on foot or horseback, taking part in relays up to 250 miles (402 km) each day.

> **In Cathay, everyone writes his name, that of each family member, and how many horses he has on the door of his house, so the governor of each city knows how many people live there.**

so that the dead person's spirit would be able to "own" all these things in the next world.

ENVIRONMENTS

Polo memorized details of local environments, noting landscape, vegetation, weather, wildlife, and all the useful crops that were grown there. In southern China, he saw vast quantities of ginger and rice being harvested. In India, he saw cotton, sugar-cane, and spices unknown in Europe.

In Sumatra, he saw apes and monkeys. In Burma, he marveled at giant oxen and elephants. In India, he admired panthers and parrots, remarking that there was "no lovelier sight in the world."

When commenting on climates, he described the air in the mountains between China and Burma as "unwholesome and pestilent," and the southern Indian climate as "scarcely tolerable," claiming that river water was hot enough in places to boil an egg. In the Persian Gulf region, he admired houses built with special ventilators designed to circulate cooling drafts in the overpowering heat.

EMPIRE AND BUSINESS

Polo reported to Kublai Khan about how his empire was being run, and perhaps he even spied on other officials. In his book, Polo described protests and revolts against the khan's rule. Maybe these protests arose because of high taxes imposed on the empire's most important products. Goods, such as charcoal, salt, sugar, and rice wine, yielded almost 15 million gold coins every year, making Kublai Khan incredibly rich.

GOING HOME

After 17 years in Asia, the Polos asked Kublai Khan's permission to return to Europe. At first he was reluctant, but finally he agreed, asking them to escort a Mongol princess, Kokachin, on her way to marry a Mongol ruler in the Middle East. The land route was blocked by war in Central Asia, so the Polos decided to travel by sea. They set sail in Chinese junks, among the safest and most technologically advanced ships in the world. Each junk was built with watertight bulkheads in the hull. Also, Chinese navigators used compasses, which were still unknown in Europe. Even so, the voyage was a disaster.

It took over 18 months for the Polos' fleet to cross the South China Sea, pass by the islands of Indonesia and Malaya, round the tip of India, and finally reach safe harbor in the Persian Gulf. Polo reported that among 600 passengers, only 18, plus the three Polos, survived.

TRUE OR FALSE?

In his book, Marco Polo did not mention fireworks used to celebrate the Chinese New Year (*above*), but he did describe Mongol New Year festivities at Kublai Khan's court.

Today, the Great Wall of China (*below*) is a massive monument, but the stonework admired by modern visitors is part of a repair project that began around A.D. 1480.

Marco Polo described things that he saw in his travels, but over the years, many have asked if he actually saw everything that he claimed to have seen.

During his lifetime, Marco Polo was accused of boastful exaggeration. Back home in Venice, he was given the nickname *Marco il Milione*, meaning "Marco the Million." This might refer either to the wealth he brought back from his travels or to something like "Marco of a Million Lies."

In the centuries following Marco Polo's death in 1324, historians and experts in geography, travel, and exploration have studied his text in great detail, looking for clues that might prove, once and for all, whether Polo's stories about his travels are true or false. Three main points cause concern.

First, Polo does not mention certain things about China that seem obvious or important to travelers today. He does not make any mention of tea or the Great Wall of China, for example.

> ❝ *This is a clear and ordered account as told by the wise and noble Venetian Marco Polo of things he saw himself and a few things he did not witness but which he was told by honest people.* ❞
>
> RUSTICHELLO

Second, Polo does not use many Chinese words in his text, preferring to use Turkish or Mongol names for the people and places he claimed to have visited.

Third, his text exists in several different versions, which do not all agree on certain details.

EXPLANATIONS

Most of these concerns can be explained, however. In Polo's time, the Great Wall of China was in ruins, and it would not have looked very impressive. Since the Wall had been built to keep out invading tribes but had failed to do so, it may not have seemed worth commenting on.

Also, Polo's failure to mention tea may be linked to his interest in wine, which he mentioned frequently in his book. As a traveling official, he did not spend much time eating meals in

The old Croatian town of Korcula (*below*) was a busy port in Marco Polo's time. His family owned a combination store and house in the town, and Croatian traditions has it that Polo himself was born here, but no documents survive to prove this.

In his book, Polo did not mention tea (*right*), but he did describe many foods and drinks that were unknown in Europe, including raw pork with soy sauce, camel flesh, coconuts, jujube dates, koumiss (fermented horse milk favored by the Mongols), palm-tree sap, and rice wine.

It takes many years to learn how to write Chinese characters (*right*). Polo claimed to have studied four languages on his travels, but, so far as we can tell, he never learned to read or write Chinese.

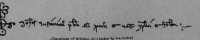

Polo's will (*left*) gives us few clues about his travels.

family homes — where most tea was drunk. Instead, he described inns and wine shops, where travelers stopped for refreshments. He also mentioned great feasts, mostly in the khan's palace, where Mongol specialities, like mare's milk, were served.

Polo probably did not use Chinese words because he did not speak Chinese. He did, however, know both Turki and the Mongol language. It seems natural that he would have used Turkish versions of place names, which members of the Mongol government he worked for would understand.

As for the inconsistent versions of the same text, when Rusticello wrote down Polo's story, his audience expected to hear romantic tales and be able to enjoy elaborate details, even if they were exaggerated. In addition, Rusticello's text became so popular that it was copied by hand over 150 times. As each scribe made copies, he added little details of his own to improve the original story or add entertainment. Rusticello's original text has not survived, making it difficult to check the other copies.

PROBABLY TRUE

In spite of some concerns, most historians think that Polo's descriptions of his travels are probably basically true. Few documents survive to confirm the details of his life, but Polo's book contains so much information about so many places that it would have been difficult for him to invent it all if he had not traveled widely. Remember, in Polo's time there were no newspapers, radios, or televisions to carry words and images around the world.

Also, Polo had no motive, apart from pride, to tell lies. He made no money from his book. Most important of all, he firmly claimed, even on his deathbed, that his stories were true. When a priest asked him to confess his sins or risk going to Hell, Polo denied that he had invented details of his adventures. Instead, he proudly stated, "I have only told the half of what I saw."

FOR FURTHER DISCUSSION

Many aspects of Polo's travels are thought to be controversial and therefore open to debate. The following questions can be used to guide classroom discussion.

1 Why do you think 17-year-old Marco Polo agreed to leave his home to travel halfway around the world to an unknown land?

2 Which part of Polo's three-year journey to China do you think was most dangerous?
- The voyage across the Mediterranean Sea to the Middle East
- The trek though hot lands beside the Persian Gulf
- Climbing over the Pamir Mountains
- Riding over the grassy plains of Central Asia
- Crossing the "haunted" Taklamakan desert

3 Why do you think Kublai Khan welcomed Polo and other foreigners to his court?

4 If you were a merchant living in the Middle East, why would Kublai Khan and his Mongol army, thousands of miles away, make a difference in your life?

5 What sort of dangers would Marco Polo have had to face in his role as a roving ambassador for the Great Khan?

6 If you were a Chinese person in one of the cities conquered by Kublai Khan, what would you think about the following features of Mongol rule?
- no jobs for Chinese scholars
- strong city gates and walls
- new rulers who do not understand Chinese civilization
- well-trained city firefighters
- new roads, canals, and bridges for transporting goods
- foreign government officials
- high taxes
- help for poor families, paid for by taxes

7 Do you think Mongol paper currency was a useful invention, or were coins better?

8 Why did Polo choose to make careful observations of all he saw on his travels?

9 Why do you think Polo and other merchants believed extraordinary tales, such as the one that tells of eagles collecting diamonds?

10 Why do you think Polo was ready to leave China and return to Europe in 1292?

11 If Marco Polo lived in the 21st century, where might he travel and why?

12 Can you sum up Marco Polo's life in 12 words or less?

MAJOR WORLD EVENTS

During Marco Polo's life and the time that he traveled to places that had probably never before been seen by Europeans, people in the rest of the world were fighting wars and attempting to expand their empires.

Find out about some of these major world events (*right*) and judge how they may have affected Polo's accomplishment.

1250 The Mameluk dynasty (former slaves) takes control of Egypt, fights Mongols, defeats Christian Crusaders, and invades rival states in the Middle East. Their rule lasts until 1300.

1258 Mongol armies capture Baghdad (now in Iraq). At the time, Baghdad was the most powerful city in Muslim lands.

1260 Kublai Khan declares himself emperor of China and founds the Yuan dynasty.

1270 Warlord Yekuno Amlak takes control of Ethiopia and sets up an empire in East Africa.

1281 Mongol armies invade Japan by sea, but they are driven back.

1291 Christian Crusaders are forced to leave the Holy Land.

1291 The country of Switzerland is founded (Swiss Confederation), making it a nation of 23 states.

1294 Kublai Khan dies.

1297 Scottish soldier William Wallace leads rebellions against English rule.

1299 Mongols invade northern India.

1300 Turkish general Osman I founds the Ottoman empire in the Middle East.

1300 The kingdom of Benin (West Africa) grows powerful.

1300 (approximately) Giant statues of gods and ancestors are carved on Easter Island in the Pacific Ocean.

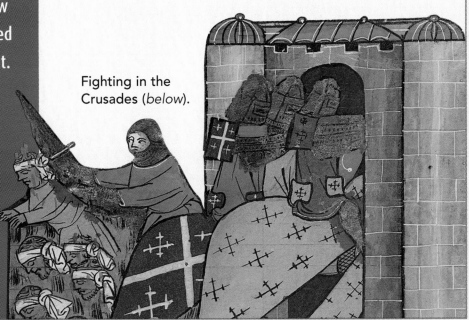

Fighting in the Crusades (*below*).

OVER THE YEARS

- Many travel agencies, hotels, restaurants, and shops selling imported goods use Marco Polo's name.

The international airport in Venice, Italy, is named after Marco Polo (*left*).

- Christopher Columbus owned a copy of Marco Polo's book, and he studied it before setting off on his voyage from Europe to the Americas in 1492.

- Chinese-American composer Tan Dun created an opera about Marco Polo's travels. It was first performed in 1996. Another musical about Polo premiered in Croatia in 2001.

- Automobile manufacturer Mercedes-Benz markets a "Marco Polo" car, designed for long-distance travels.

- Marco Polo has been pictured on postage stamps issued by many countries, including Canada, Australia, San Marino, and Italy.

- A rare breed of long-horned sheep that lives only in Central Asia is known as the "Marco Polo" sheep.

- International traders use the "Marco Polo Business Network" on the Internet to make contacts with buyers and sellers in distant lands.

- A Croatian rock group has recorded a song in praise of Marco Polo.

- In his book, Marco Polo described a magnificent stone bridge near Beijing, China, decorated with 485 carved stone lions. Today it is a popular tourist attraction and bears his name.

- The government of the People's Republic of China and Volunteers of the United States have set up a Marco Polo Award. It is presented annually to men or women who "carry on Marco Polo's spirit of goodwill" in international relations or trade.

Although many people questioned whether or not he had actually traveled to all the places he claimed, Marco Polo's adventures have inspired explorers, travelers, writers, and musicians throughout the ages.

Discover how some of his achievements have been remembered (*left*).

GLOSSARY

administrator: someone who manages or supervises.

alliance: bond between two groups to further a common interest.

Buddhism: a religious faith that grew out of the teachings of Gautama Buddha.

bulkhead: a wall dividing the hull of a ship into separate watertight compartments.

Byzantium: a rich and powerful city whose rulers controlled an empire in eastern Europe and the Middle East. Today, known as Istanbul.

Christian: one who believes in the teachings of Jesus Christ.

cobalt: a metallic element that can be used to make a blue dye.

commodity: something useful or of value.

cowrie shells: glossy, brightly colored shells.

desolate: uninhabited.

dynasty: a succession of rulers from the same family.

exotic: from a distant land.

expedition: a long journey taken for a specific purpose.

exuberant: joyous and enthusiastic.

falconers: people who care for and hunt with hawks.

flint: a hard rock that produces a spark when struck.

gilded: covered with a thin coating of gold.

Great Wall of China: a massive wall first built around 200 B.C. to protect northern China from invasions.

hinder: to delay or get in the way of.

hostels: inns or other places to stay.

inhospitable: showing no friendliness.

interpreters: people who explain or tell the meaning of something in a different language.

Islam: the religious faith of Muslims.

javelins: light spears thrown as weapons or for hunting.

jujube dates: fruit produced by trees in the buckthorn family.

khan: a title used by Mongol rulers.

Kurdish: relating to the people who live in a plateau region of the Middle East.

lacquered: coated with the varnish known as lacquer.

loincloth: cloth worn in warm climates that only covers the private parts of the body.

looted: stolen during times of unrest.

malaria: a disease of chills and fevers caused by a parasite that is carried by mosquitoes.

millet: a grain that is eaten.

mirages: the effect of light rays that bend as they pass through layers of hot, dry air, causing non-existant images of such things as pools of water.

mirth: happiness.

money changers: those who exchange one kind of money for another.

Mongols: an Asian group of people originally from Mongolia.

monks: men of a certain religion who live in a monastery.

Muslims: people who follow the teachings of Muhammad and the faith of Islam.

nobleman: a man born into a privileged family.

nomads: people who do not live in one place but who move their homes from place to place.

novelties: new or unusual things.

oases: green fertile areas surrounded by desert.

oxygen shortage: can cause illness in people in high altitude, where the atmosphere contains less oxygen than it does at ground level.

passport: official document carried by travelers to prove their identity.

pestilent: destructive or causing displeasure.

philosophy: a search for a general understanding of values.

physiques: the structures of people's bodies.

plateau: an area of high, flat land.

pope: the leader of the Roman Catholic Church.

rivalry: a competition.

ruddy: having a reddish color.

rukh (or roc): a legendary giant bird that is mentioned in both Marco Polo's book and in tales from the *Arabian Nights*, a famous collection of Middle Eastern tales.

scholarship: qualities of learning.

scribe: a copier of manuscripts.

sepulcher: a place of burial or a tomb.

shamans: priests who use magic for curing.

shrewd: being aware of or clever in figuring things out.

strenuous: vigorous, requiring a great deal of effort.

sultan: a ruler of a Muslim state.

thresh: to separate the seeds from the plant.

traders: people whose business it is to buy and sell goods.

Venetian: relating to Venice, Italy.

yogi: an Indian holy man.

FOR FURTHER STUDY

BOOKS

Marco Polo. Charles Parlin Graves
(Chelsea House)

Marco Polo. Struan Reid (Heinemann Library)

Marco Polo: A Journey Through China.
Fiona MacDonald (Franklin Watts)

Marco Polo and the Medieval Explorers.
Rebecca Stefoff (Chelsea House)

Marco Polo and the Wonders of the East.
Hal Marcovitz (Chelsea House)

Marco Polo for Kids. Janis Herbert
(Chicago Review Press)

*Marco Polo: Marco Polo and the Silk Road
to China*. Michael Burgan
(Compass Point Books)

Travels of Marco Polo. Alex Bandon
(Raintree Steck-Vaughn)

World in the Time of Marco Polo.
Fiona MacDonald (Chelsea House)

VIDEOS

Biography: Marco Polo.
(A&E Entertainment)

*History's Mysteries: The True Story
of Marco Polo.* (A&E Home Video)

WEB SITES

Marco Polo.
**www.nationalgeographic.com/ngm/0105/
feature1/**

Mysteries of History.
**www.usnews.com/usnews/doubleissue/
mysteries/marco.htm**

Marco Polo and His Travels.
www.silk-road.com/artl/marcopolo.shtml

Marco Polo & Korcula.
www.korcula.net/mpolo/index.html